Isaac Asimov's
21st Century
Library of the
Universe

The Solar System

Jupiter

BY ISAAC ASIMOV
WITH REVISIONS AND UPDATING BY RICHARD HANTULA

Gareth Stevens Publishing
A WORLD ALMANAC EDUCATION GROUP COMPANY

Please visit our web site at: www.garethstevens.com
For a free color catalog describing Gareth Stevens Publishing's list of high-quality
books and multimedia programs, call 1-800-542-2595 (USA) or 1-800-387-3178 (Canada).
Gareth Stevens Publishing's fax: (414) 332-3567.

The reproduction rights to all photographs and illustrations in this book are controlled by the individuals
or institutions credited on page 32 and may not be reproduced without their permission.

Library of Congress Cataloging-in-Publication Data

Asimov, Isaac.
    Jupiter / by Isaac Asimov; with revisions and updating by Richard Hantula.
       p. cm. — (Isaac Asimov's 21st century library of the universe. The solar system)
    Rev. ed. of: Planet of extremes: Jupiter. 1995.
    Summary: A description of Jupiter, the largest planet in our solar system, which includes
information on its numerous moons, space probes which have studied it, and the 1994 collision
of comet remnants with the planet.
    Includes bibliographical references and index.
    ISBN 0-8368-3235-3 (lib. bdg.)
    1. Jupiter (Planet)—Juvenile literature. [1. Jupiter (Planet).] I. Hantula, Richard. II. Asimov, Isaac.
Planet of extremes. III. Title. IV. Isaac Asimov's 21st century library of the universe. Solar system.
QB661.A845   2002
523.45—dc21   2002021778

This edition first published in 2002 by
Gareth Stevens Publishing
A World Almanac Education Group Company
330 West Olive Street, Suite 100
Milwaukee, WI 53212 USA

Series editor: Betsy Rasmussen
Cover design and layout adaptation: Melissa Valuch
Picture research: Matthew Groshek
Additional picture research: Diane Laska-Swanke
Production director: Susan Ashley

The editors at Gareth Stevens Publishing have selected science author Richard Hantula to bring
this classic series of young people's information books up to date. Richard Hantula has written
and edited books and articles on science and technology for more than two decades. He was
the senior U.S. editor for the *Macmillan Encyclopedia of Science*.

In addition to Hantula's contribution to this most recent edition, the editors would like to
acknowledge the participation of two noted science authors, Greg Walz-Chojnacki and
Francis Reddy, as contributors to earlier editions of this work.

Printed in the United States of America

1 2 3 4 5 6 7 8 9 06 05 04 03 02

Contents

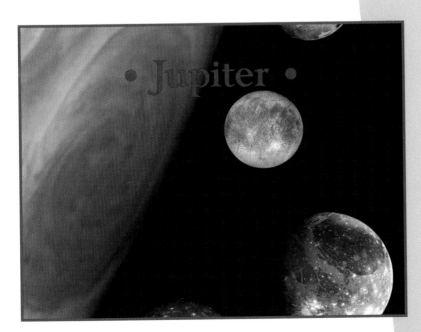

We live in an enormously large place – the Universe. It is only natural that we would want to understand this place, so scientists and engineers have developed instruments and spacecrafts that have told us far more about the Universe than we could possibly imagine.

We have seen planets up close, and spacecrafts have even landed on some. We have learned about quasars and pulsars, super-novas and colliding galaxies, and black holes and dark matter. We have gathered amazing data about how the Universe may have come into being and how it may end. Nothing could be more astonishing.

Jupiter, named for the king of the gods in ancient Roman myths, is the largest planet in our Solar System. Jupiter is an enormous world that dwarfs our own Earth. In fact, nearly everything about the planet is extreme – its atmosphere, its storms, its temperatures, and its collection of moons, where you can find fiery volcanoes, icy plains, and perhaps even salty oceans. Scientists have learned much about Jupiter and its moons in recent years, thanks to the spacecrafts that have explored it.

The Bright Planet Jupiter

Jupiter is usually the fourth-brightest object in the sky. Only the Sun, Earth's Moon, and Venus are always brighter. Mars, when it is at its brightest, is also brighter than Jupiter.

In 1610, Italian scientist Galileo Galilei looked at Jupiter through a small telescope. Near the planet, he saw four dimmer objects. Night after night, the objects moved back and forth from one side of Jupiter to the other.

These objects turned out to be moons, or natural satellites, of Jupiter. They circle Jupiter the way our Moon circles Earth.

Above: A portrait of Galileo.

Above: Galileo's sketches of Jupiter and three of the four moons he observed.

4

Galileo viewed Jupiter's four biggest moons through his homemade telescopes (shown here mounted on a special stand in a museum). Today, these moons can be seen with a good pair of binoculars *(inset)*.

A clear night and a good pair of binoculars or a telescope are needed to spot Jupiter with its moons.

Jupiter and its four largest moons as seen through a small telescope.

Seeing Jupiter

Jupiter orbits the Sun about once every 12 years. It stays in the zodiac. The zodiac is an imaginary belt in the sky containing the paths of the Sun, our Moon, and most of the planets. The zodiac is divided into 12 equal parts. Each part is named for a constellation.

When Jupiter is viewed through a small telescope or a good pair of binoculars, it looks like a little disk of light. Nearby are Jupiter's four largest satellites, some on one side of the planet, some on the other. From night to night, the positions of the satellites change as they move around Jupiter.

Left: Jupiter and its four largest moons, viewed over the course of eight straight nights. The moons seem to play hide-and-seek as they circle their parent planet.

A Closer Look

With a diameter of 88,846 miles (142,984 kilometers) at its equator, Jupiter is the biggest planet in our Solar System. It is more than 11 times wider than Earth, and it has the volume of 1,300 Earths. Even though Jupiter is so large, it spins much faster than Earth spins. Earth makes one full turn on its axis in 24 hours. Jupiter makes a full turn in just under 10 hours.

Scientists have received lots of data and close-up photographs of Jupiter from spacecrafts that have explored the planet. The spacecrafts *Pioneer 10*, *Pioneer 11*, *Voyager 1*, *Voyager 2*, and *Cassini* flew past Jupiter, and the spacecraft *Galileo* sent a probe into the planet's atmosphere. They found the planet is a huge ball made up mainly of the two simplest gases — mostly hydrogen plus some helium. The atmosphere also has vapors of substances such as water, methane, and ammonia.

Right: Jupiter outweighs all the other planets in the Solar System put together.

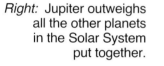

The heavyweight champ of the Solar System

Jupiter is so large that it is more than three times as massive as Saturn, the next largest planet. Imagine you have a huge scale. Now put Jupiter in one of the pans of the scale. In the other pan, imagine you pile up all the other planets, satellites, asteroids, and comets. All of them put together would not balance the scale. Jupiter is more than twice as massive as all the other known planetary material in the Solar System put together!

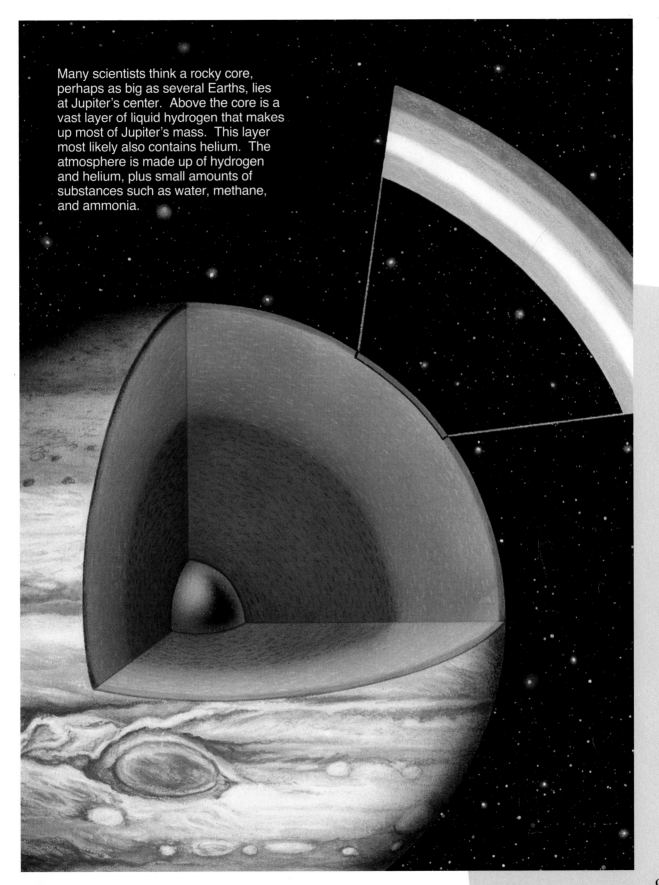

Many scientists think a rocky core, perhaps as big as several Earths, lies at Jupiter's center. Above the core is a vast layer of liquid hydrogen that makes up most of Jupiter's mass. This layer most likely also contains helium. The atmosphere is made up of hydrogen and helium, plus small amounts of substances such as water, methane, and ammonia.

Jupiter's Great Red Spot *(left)* and a storm on Earth *(right)* are similar in appearance, but not in size.

Above: The Great Red Spot is huge, but it appears to be shrinking. Near the end of the twentieth century, it measured about 7,500 miles (12,000 km) from north to south and about 15,500 miles (25,000 km) from east to west, or roughly about the same as two Earths side by side. A century earlier, it was about 25,000 miles (40,000 km) wide — bigger than three Earths!

The Great Red Spot

Jupiter's surface is covered with dark "belts," with lighter "zones" between them. These areas are created by atmospheric movements. Vast winds move downward in the belts and upward in the zones.

Along the belts and zones are light and dark oval spots that are actually enormous whirling storm winds. The largest of these is called the Great Red Spot. It looks like a gigantic tornado or hurricane that never stops. Astronomers have watched it whirling for over 300 years.

A storm with a mind of its own?

Many mysteries surround the Great Red Spot. For one thing, scientists are not certain why it has lasted for centuries. Other storms come and go, but the Great Red Spot seems to be almost permanent. Scientists also wonder about the Great Red Spot's change in size and about its movements. It can move ahead or fall behind the surrounding clouds. It moves east and west, but not north and south.

Rings around the Planet

All four of our Solar System's "giant" planets — Jupiter, Saturn, Uranus, and Neptune — have rings made up of very small pieces of material. Each planet's assortment of rings is different.

Saturn's rings, which consist largely of chunks of ice, are bright and very large. Astronomers have known about them since the 1600s. Galileo, using his telescope, was the first to see that Saturn was more than just a disk. He noticed it had strange additions, although he did not realize they were rings.

Jupiter's rings are dim and small, however, and seem to be made mainly of dust. Astronomers did not find out about them until the late twentieth century.

In 1979, the *Voyager 1* probe discovered a thin ring about 30,000 miles (48,000 km) above Jupiter's cloud tops. Pictures later made by *Voyager 2* and *Galileo* showed that there was more than just a single slim ring. Within the inside edge of this main ring, which is only about 4,300 miles (7,000 km) wide, there is a cloudlike ring known as the halo. Two very faint "gossamer" rings extend out beyond the main ring.

The rings are constantly being fed by dust coming from four tiny moons that lie in or next to the rings. These moons are called Metis, Adrastea, Amalthea, and Thebe. The dust is blasted off the moons when they are hit by meteorites.

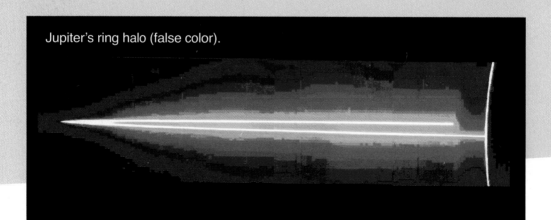
Jupiter's ring halo (false color).

Above: Jupiter's inner satellites and ring components, based on *Galileo* findings and produced in 1998.

Main ring of Jupiter.

The Moons of Jupiter

Jupiter has many moons. At least 16 have been officially confirmed and given names. Of these, the four largest are sometimes called the Galilean satellites in honor of Galileo. The four satellites' names were proposed by a German astronomer, Simon Marius, who claimed he spotted them a short time before Galileo did. The Galilean moon nearest to Jupiter is Io. Beyond Io are Europa, Ganymede, and Callisto. Europa is slightly smaller than Earth's Moon, and the other three are larger.

Closer to Jupiter than its four big satellites are the four small moons connected with the planet's rings. The other confirmed moons lie beyond the orbits of the Galilean satellites. They range in size from about 6 to 106 miles (10 to 170 km) across. The most distant, Sinope, is 14,700,000 miles (23,700,000 km) from Jupiter, on average. At least some of these moons are probably captured asteroids.

Below and opposite, inset: Who's who in the Jupiter system? The orbits of Jupiter's 16 confirmed moons, big and small, are shown.

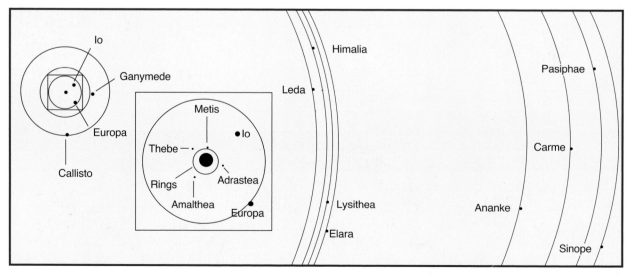

A set of pictures of Jupiter
and the Galilean satellites
made by *Voyager 1* in 1979
(the images are not to scale).
Clockwise from upper right:
Europa, Ganymede, Callisto,
Jupiter, and Io.

The icy, fractured surface of Callisto, photographed by *Voyager 1* in 1979. Notice the bright ringed region near the moon's left edge — the remains of a violent impact that partially melted Callisto's frozen surface. This region is about 190 miles (300 km) across.

Icy and Cratered Callisto

Callisto, the farthest of the Galilean satellites from Jupiter, is 1,170,000 miles (1,883,000 km) from the planet. That is almost five times as far as our Moon is from Earth. Callisto orbits Jupiter in about 16 $\frac{2}{3}$ days.

Probes have shown that Callisto is a big ball of ice with some rock, and it may have a rocky core. It has a very thin atmosphere made up of the gas carbon dioxide. Some scientists think a salty ocean might lie beneath the moon's icy crust.

Callisto is heavily covered with craters, made by the impacts of objects from space. Most of the craters do not seem to be very deep. This may be because the icy surface slowly flowed and settled, but the flow was not enough to eliminate the craters entirely.

Left: A *Galileo* close-up of Callisto's heavily cratered landscape illustrates the point that Callisto has lots of large and small craters.

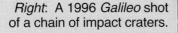

Right: A 1996 *Galileo* shot of a chain of impact craters.

An artist's view of Jupiter from Ganymede, the largest satellite in our Solar System.

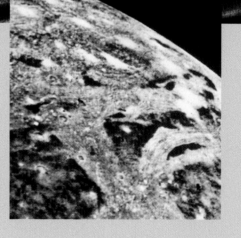

Right: The terrain of Ganymede is grooved. Scientists think the grooves are caused by slow expansion and movement of the moon's crust.

The Solar System's Largest Moon – Ganymede

Ganymede, the largest moon in the Solar System, is 3,273 miles (5,268 km) across. It is bigger than the planets Mercury and Pluto. Ganymede is 665,000 miles (1,070,000 km) from Jupiter and takes just over a week to orbit the planet.

Like Callisto, Ganymede seems to be mostly ice with some rock, and it may possibly have a liquid ocean below its surface. It has a thin atmosphere of oxygen. Ganymede is not as thickly covered with craters as Callisto. That may be because Ganymede's crust seems to have cracked and shifted in many places over a long period of time. Perhaps water from inside Ganymede welled up, flooded many craters, and then froze smoothly over the surface.

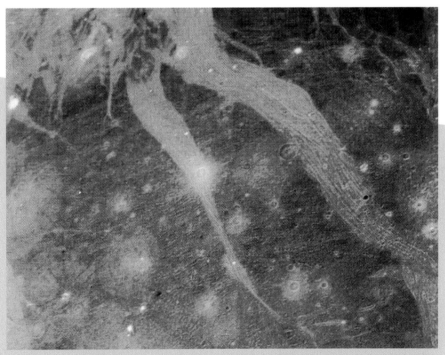

Above: Craters old and new on Ganymede. The bright patches are fresh craters. The fainter circular markings may be ancient craters smoothed over by glacierlike flows on Ganymede's icy surface.

Fire and Ice: Two Volcanic Worlds

Io and Europa are the Galilean moons closest to Jupiter. Both are stretched slightly by the huge planet's gravity, and this creates heat. Both moons are volcanic. Io erupts with molten rock, Europa with water.

Io is a rocky world a bit bigger than Earth's Moon. It orbits Jupiter every $1^3/4$ days at a distance of about 262,000 miles (421,600 km) from the planet. The moon's inner rock is heated by the action of Jupiter's powerful magnetic field as well as by the planet's gravity. The rock melts and eventually explodes out in eruptions that shoot gas and yellow sulfur high into the sky. Io has an atmosphere made of sulfur dioxide. With its hundreds of volcanoes, it is the most volcanically active world in our Solar System.

Europa, the smallest of the Galilean moons, is about 1,945 miles (3,130 km) across. It lies about 416,900 miles (670,900 km) from Jupiter and completes one orbit every $3^1/2$ days. It is covered with a rather smooth layer of ice, below which there seems to be a sea of water. Any craters formed by meteorites on the surface are filled by water that comes up from below and freezes. Europa has a thin oxygen atmosphere, and some scientists wonder if the moon's sea could contain life as we know it. So far, however, there is no evidence for this.

Io volcano eruptions. *Above, left:* A 1996 Hubble Space Telescope picture showing 249-mile-tall (400-km-tall) eruption from volcano Pele in silhouette against the bluish disk of Jupiter. *Above, right:* Volcano Culann Patera as imaged by *Galileo* in November 1999.

Europa's rather smooth, icy surface is covered with dark streaks. Scientists think they are cracks produced by the pull of Jupiter's powerful gravity. The dark color may be due to substances carried up through the cracks by water rising from below.

21

Probing the Planet Jupiter

Space probes, the Hubble Space Telescope, and Earth-based instruments have given astronomers much information about Jupiter. We now know that Jupiter is surrounded by a magnetic field much larger and stronger than Earth's. The field is so strong and collects so many charged particles that it will be necessary for spaceships with humans aboard to stay far away from Jupiter unless protective measures are taken. Around the planet's magnetic poles, the magnetic field draws particles into the upper atmosphere, making the atmosphere's gases glow in brilliant auroras.

The probes have also revealed that although temperatures surrounding Jupiter's cloud layer are very low, temperatures rise rapidly beneath the clouds. Thousands of miles below the cloud layer, Jupiter is hotter than the surface of the Sun!

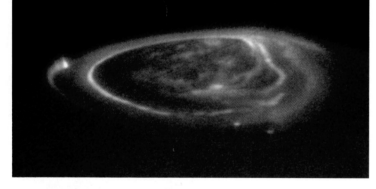

A 1998 Hubble Space Telescope image of Jupiter's aurora.

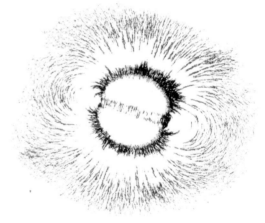

Above: A magnetic field can be visualized by placing a magnet under a sheet of paper covered with iron filings.

Jupiter — brought to you in living color

Jupiter is a very colorful planet. The belts are orange, yellow, and brown. There are white spots and, of course, the Great Red Spot, which is not always red. Sometimes, the Great Red Spot's color pales until it can hardly be seen. Scientists are not certain what chemical reactions cause all the colors.

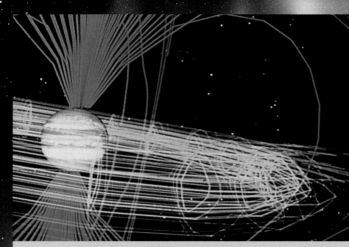

A computer image of Jupiter's intense magnetic field *(in blue)*. Also shown is a trail of sulfur *(in yellow)* left by Io, a volcanic moon of Jupiter.

An artist's conception of a spectacular display in Jupiter's nighttime sky. The fierce lightning and streamers of light surpass in size and brilliance anything likely to be seen in Earth's atmosphere.

Galileo's Epic Voyage

The spacecraft *Galileo* was launched toward Jupiter in 1989. The mission seemed to be ruined when an important antenna failed to open completely, but engineers figured out how to make a less powerful antenna on the craft send the data.

Galileo followed a roundabout route to Jupiter in order to use the gravity of Venus and Earth to boost its speed. In 1991, it took the first close-up pictures of an asteroid, Gaspra. A couple of years later, pictures it took of another asteroid, Ida, provided the first proof that an asteroid could have a moon. Finally, in 1995, *Galileo* arrived at Jupiter.

The spacecraft dropped a probe into the planet's atmosphere and then explored the giant planet and some of its moons. Among the craft's many discoveries were Jupiter's gossamer rings. By early 2002, *Galileo*'s fuel was nearly used up. Mission controllers on Earth left the spacecraft on a course that was expected to take it, in 2003, into Jupiter's atmosphere, where it would vaporize.

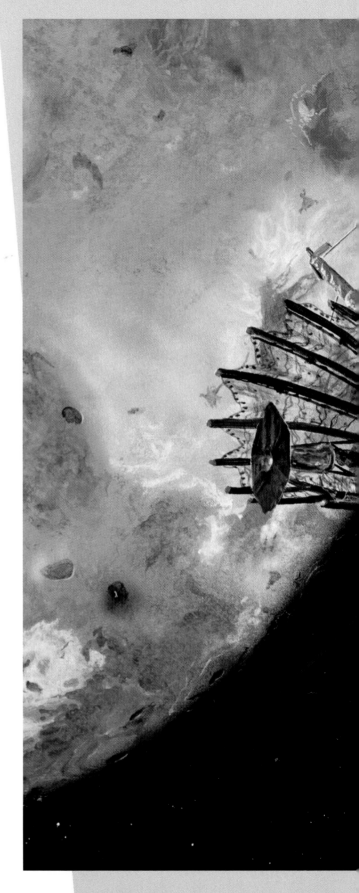

Galileo has made a looping journey around Jupiter and its moons. This drawing shows the probe, with its malfunctioning antenna, on a visit to Io.

Smash Hits:
A Comet Collides with Jupiter

A comet called Shoemaker-Levy 9 came so close to Jupiter in 1992 that it was broken up by the planet's powerful gravity into 21 pieces. In July 1994, these pieces smashed into Jupiter. Tremendous explosions "excavated" the cloud tops, giving astronomers another way to see what lies below.

The comet pieces struck on the side of Jupiter not visible from Earth. As the planet turned, however, the areas the comet hit came into view. Using telescopes, astronomers could see the dark "bruises" the collisions created on Jupiter. Even the spacecraft *Galileo* got into the act. It was on the far side of the planet and actually observed one of the explosions.

Left: The spacecraft *Galileo* took these four snapshots when comet pieces struck Jupiter on July 22, 1994. The photos capture the moment when the final large fragment called *W* impacted.

Jupiter's center — almost an inner Sun?

Scientists think most of Jupiter is made up mainly of hydrogen and helium. At its center, the planet probably has a rocky core that may be as big as several Earths. The center squeezed so hard that considerable heat is produced there, although the temperature does not get as high as inside the Sun, where heat results from nuclear fusion. Still, Jupiter produces more heat than it receives from the Sun.

An artist's view of comet fragments hitting Jupiter's cloud tops.

One of Jupiter's "black eyes" made by a fragment of a comet.

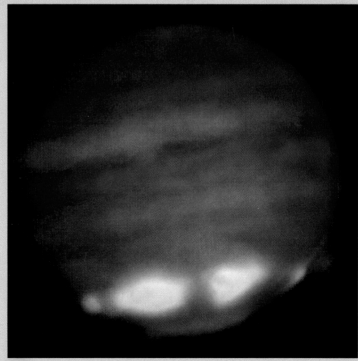

Above: In this infrared, or "heat," image, the bright spots reveal where comet fragments struck Jupiter.

Jupiter

Left and Below: A close-up of Jupiter and its seven largest moons *(below, left to right)*, Himalia, Callisto, Ganymede, Europa, Io, Thebe, and Amalthea (not shown in the same scale as the planet).

Confirmed, Named Moons of Jupiter

Name	Metis	Adrastea	Amalthea	Thebe	Io	Europa
Diameter *	25 miles (40 km)	16 miles (25 km)	106 miles (179 km)	62 miles (100 km)	2,263 miles (3,643 km)	1,945 miles (3,130 km)
Distance from Jupiter **	79,511 miles (127,960 km)	80,144 miles (128,980 km)	112,700 miles (181,300 km)	137,900 miles (221,900 km)	262,000 miles (421,600 km)	416,900 miles (670,900 km)
Name	**Ganymede**	**Callisto**	**Leda**	**Himalia**	**Lysithea**	**Elara**
Diameter *	3,273 miles (5,268 km)	2,986 miles (4,806 km)	6 miles (10 km)	106 miles (170 km)	15 miles (24 km)	50 miles (80 km)
Distance from Jupiter **	665,000 miles (1,070,000 km)	1,170,000 miles (1,883,000 km)	6,893,000 miles (11,094,000 km)	7,133,000 miles (11,480,000 km)	7,282,000 miles (11,720,000 km)	7,293,000 miles (11,737,000 km)
Name	**Ananke**	**Carme**	**Pasiphae**	**Sinope**		
Diameter *	12 miles (20 km)	19 miles (30 km)	22 miles (36 km)	17 miles (28 km)		
Distance from Jupiter **	13,170,000 miles (21,200,000 km)	14,040,000 miles (22,600,000 km)	14,600,000 miles (23,500,000 km)	14,700,000 miles (23,700,000 km)		

* Average width

** Average distance from Jupiter's center

Fact File:
Jupiter, the Largest Planet

The Sun and its Solar System (*left to right*): Mercury, Venus, Earth, Mars, Jupiter, Saturn, Uranus, Neptune, Pluto.

Our Solar System's largest-known planet, Jupiter, is the fifth-closest to the Sun. Like the Sun, Jupiter is mostly hydrogen and helium. Scientists believe the temperature at its core might be higher than 36,000° F (20,000° C). When it was formed over 4.5 billion years ago, Jupiter probably gave off substantially more energy than it does now. Jupiter was never massive enough to begin the process of nuclear fusion that stars use to burn their hydrogen, but billions of years ago, it might have glowed like a star!

Jupiter:
How It Measures Up to Earth

Planet	Diameter*	Rotation Period (length of day)	Period of Orbit around Sun (length of year)	Known Moons	Surface Gravity
Jupiter	88,846 miles (142,984 km)	9 hours, 56 minutes	11.86 years	16+**	2.36***
Earth	7,927 miles (12,756 km)	23 hours, 56 minutes	365.256 days (1 year)	1	1.00***

Planet	Distance from Sun (nearest–farthest)	Least Time It Takes for Light to Travel to Earth
Jupiter	460.1–507.4 million miles (740.5–816.6 million km)	32.7 minutes
Earth	91.3–94.4 million miles (147–152 million km)	—

* Diameter at the equator.

** Over three dozen moons have been reportedly observed around Jupiter; of them, at least 16 have been confirmed and given names.

*** Multiply your weight by this number to find out how much you would weigh on this planet; in the case of Jupiter, which lacks a surface, the number is for cloud-top level.

More Books about Jupiter

Destination: Jupiter. Seymour Simon (HarperTrophy)

DK Space Encyclopedia. Nigel Henbest and Heather Couper (DK Publishing)

Galileo Spacecraft: Mission to Jupiter. Michael D. Cole (Enslow)

A Look at Jupiter. Ray Spangenburg and Kit Moser (Franklin Watts)

Jupiter. Larry Dane Brimner (Children's Press)

Jupiter. Robin Kerrod (Lerner)

Jupiter. Elaine Landau (Franklin Watts)

Jupiter: The Fifth Planet. Michael D. Cole (Enslow)

CD-ROMs and DVDs

CD-ROM: *Exploring the Planets.* (Cinegram)

DVD: *The Voyager Odyssey: An Interplanetary Music Video Experience.*
(Image Entertainment)

Web Sites

The Internet is a good place to get more information about Jupiter. The web sites listed here can help you learn about the most recent discoveries, as well as those made in the past.

Galileo: Journey to Jupiter. www.jpl.nasa.gov/galileo/

Nine Planets. www.nineplanets.org/jupiter.html

Pioneer Missions. spaceprojects.arc.nasa.gov/Space_Projects/pioneer/PN10&11.html

Views of the Solar System. www.solarviews.com/eng/jupiter.htm

Voyager. voyager.jpl.nasa.gov/

Windows to the Universe. www.windows.ucar.edu/tour/link=/jupiter/jupiter.html

Places to Visit

Here are some museums and centers where you can find a variety of space exhibits.

American Museum of Natural History
Central Park West at 79th Street
New York, NY 10024

Canada Science and Technology Museum
1867 S. Laurent Boulevard
100 Queen's Park
Ottawa, Ontario K1G 5A3
Canada

National Air and Space Museum
Smithsonian Institution
7th and Independence Avenue SW
Washington, DC 20560

Odyssium
11211 142nd Street
Edmonton, Alberta T5M 4A1
Canada

Sydney Observatory
Observatory Hill
Spotswood
Sydney, New South Wales 2000
Australia

U.S. Space and Rocket Center
1 Tranquility Base
Huntsville, AL 35807

Glossary

asteroids: very small "planets." Hundreds of thousands of them exist in our Solar System. Most of them orbit the Sun between Mars and Jupiter.

atmosphere: the gases surrounding a planet, star, or moon.

axis: the imaginary straight line around which a planet, star, or moon turns or spins.

comet: an object made of ice, rock, and gas. It has a vapor trail that can be seen when it orbits close to the Sun.

constellation: a grouping of stars that seems to trace a familiar pattern or figure. Constellations are often named after the shapes they resemble.

crater: a hole in a surface caused by the impact of an object or a volcanic explosion.

equator: an imaginary line around the middle of a planet that is always an equal distance from the two poles of the planet. The equator divides the planet into two half-spheres, or hemispheres.

Galilean satellites: Jupiter's four largest moons – Io, Europa, Ganymede, and Callisto – which Galileo studied with his telescope.

Galileo: an Italian astronomer who developed the use of the telescope to study the Universe.

Galileo: a spacecraft launched in 1989 that began exploring Jupiter and its moons in 1995.

gravity: the force that causes objects like the Sun and its planets to be attracted to one another.

Great Red Spot: the largest of the huge whirling storms that move along the "belts" and "zones" of Jupiter.

helium: a light, colorless gas found on Jupiter.

Hubble Space Telescope: an artificial satellite carrying a telescope and related instruments that has orbited Earth since 1990.

hydrogen: a colorless, odorless gas.

moon: a small body in space that moves in an orbit around a larger body.

A moon is said to be a satellite of the larger body.

rings: bands made up of small pieces of material that circle some planets at their equators.

Solar System: the Sun with the planets and other bodies, such as asteroids, that orbit the Sun.

sulfur: a pale yellow, nonmetallic element that is used in the medical, chemical, and paper industries.

vapor: a gas formed from a solid or liquid. On Earth, clouds are made of water vapor.

zodiac: the band of 12 constellations across the sky that represents the paths of the Sun, the Moon, and all the planets except Pluto.

Index

Born in 1920, Isaac Asimov came to the United States as a young boy from his native Russia. As a young man, he was a student of biochemistry. In time, he became one of the most productive writers the world has ever known. His books cover a spectrum of topics, including science, history, language theory, fantasy, and science fiction. His brilliant imagination gained him the respect and admiration of adults and children alike. Sadly, Isaac Asimov died shortly after the publication of the first edition of *Isaac Asimov's Library of the Universe.*

The publishers wish to thank the following for permission to reproduce copyright material: front cover, 3, 17 (left), 20 (right), National Space Science Data Center and the Team Leader, Dr. Michael J. S. Belton, The Galileo Project; 4 (both), 5 (large), AIP Niels Bohr Library; 5 (inset), Courtesy of Celestron International; 6, © Richard Baum 1988; 6-7, © Garret Moore 1988; 7, © Richard Baum 1988; 8, 9, © Lynette Cook 1988; 10, NASA; 10-11, © John Foster 1988; 12, NASA; 13 (upper), NASA/JPL; 13 (lower), NASA; 14, Sabine Huschke/© Gareth Stevens, Inc.; 15 (large), NASA; 15 (inset), © George Peirson 1988; 16, Jet Propulsion Laboratory; 17 (right), NASA/JPL; 18 (upper), © Ron Miller; 18 (lower), Jet Propulsion Laboratory; 19, NASA; 20 (left), John Spencer (Lowell Observatory) and NASA; 21, NASA; 22 (left), NASA and John Clarke (University of Michigan); 22 (right), Matthew Groshek/© Gareth Stevens, Inc.; 23 (large), © John Foster 1988; 23 (inset), NASA; 24-25, © Michael Carroll; 26, NASA/JPL; 27 (upper), © Michael Carroll; 27 (lower left), Space Telescope Science Institute; 27 (lower right), European Southern Observatory (ESO); 28, © Sally Bensusen 1988; 28-29, © Sally Bensusen 1987.

Flicka, Ricka, Dicka and
THE THREE KITTENS

By

Maj Lindman

ALBERT WHITMAN
& CO

Chicago Illinois

1946

THE FLICKA, RICKA, DICKA BOOKS
By Maj Lindman

FLICKA, RICKA, DICKA AND A LITTLE DOG
FLICKA, RICKA, DICKA, AND THE STRAWBERRIES
FLICKA, RICKA, DICKA, AND THEIR NEW FRIEND
FLICKA, RICKA, DICKA, AND THE NEW DOTTED DRESSES
FLICKA, RICKA, DICKA, AND THE GIRL NEXT DOOR
FLICKA, RICKA, DICKA, AND THE THREE KITTENS

THE SNIPP, SNAPP, SNURR BOOKS
By Maj Lindman

SNIPP, SNAPP, SNURR AND THE RED SHOES
SNIPP, SNAPP, SNURR AND THE GINGERBREAD
SNIPP, SNAPP, SNURR AND THE MAGIC HORSE
SNIPP, SNAPP, SNURR AND THE BUTTERED BREAD
SNIPP, SNAPP, SNURR AND THE YELLOW SLED
SNIPP, SNAPP, SNURR AND THE BIG SURPRISE

Lithographed in the U. S. A.

Mitzi walked between them, purring.

ONE sunny afternoon Flicka, Ricka, and Dicka were walking down the street, hand in hand.

Mother had told them that they might go to see Uncle Jon and Aunt Helga who lived in a little yellow house not far away.

Mitzi, a big black-and-white cat, lived in the little yellow house with them.

As the three little girls came along, they saw Aunt Helga, Uncle Jon, and Mitzi standing in front of the little yellow house.

Aunt Helga had on her hat. A coat and pocketbook were on her arm. Uncle Jon wore his hat and overcoat. Beside him was a traveling bag.

Mitzi walked between them purring, just as though she knew they were going away and were very sorry to leave her.

AS the three little girls ran up, Flicka asked, "Where are you going?"

"We must go to our daughter," Aunt Helga told them. "We must leave at once. But what can we do with Mitzi? She will be hungry, and there will be no one to give her milk or fish."

"Come, come," said Uncle Jon, "we'll be gone only a few days, and Mitzi can catch mice."

"There's not a mouse about the house!" said Aunt Helga.

"Can't we give Mitzi her milk and fish?" asked Ricka as she took the cat in her arms. "We'd like to."

"Will you, dears?" said Aunt Helga smiling. "Here's the key to the house, and some money to buy milk and fish. We'd be greatly obliged to you."

Flicka took the key and the money.

Flicka took the key and the money

WE will take good care of Mitzi," said Dicka. "We'll buy her fresh milk and fish every day. We'll play with her, too. She won't be lonely. We'll all have fun."

"Thank you, girls," said Uncle Jon. "I feel much better about going away now, myself!"

"It is late," said Aunt Helga. "We must hurry to the train. Will you girls get a pitcher in the house and buy some fresh milk for Mitzi right away? She needs fish for supper, too."

"Of course we will," Flicka, Ricka, and Dicka answered.

Aunt Helga and Uncle Jon hurried away. The three little girls found the pitcher. Then they took it to be filled with fresh milk for Mitzi.

The three little girls took it to be filled with fresh milk.

FLICKA paid for the milk, and Ricka carried the pitcher carefully.

They saw a woman in a striped apron selling fish across the street. "We should like to buy a fish," said Flicka.

"Which fish do you want?" asked the woman in the striped apron.

"We don't want a big fish," said Flicka.

"And we certainly don't want a little fish," said Ricka, "for Mitzi is a big cat."

"Why not get a middle-sized, flat fish for your cat?" suggested the woman. "How much can you spend?"

Flicka showed her a coin, and the woman picked out a fish. Flicka paid for it and Dicka carried it to the little yellow house where Mitzi lived.

Flicka showed her a coin.

MITZI stood waiting for them at the door. Ricka got a saucer and filled it full of milk. She set it on the floor. Then Dicka put the fish on the ground.

"Let us see which Mitzi eats first," said Flicka. "That will show whether she likes milk or fish best."

Mitzi sniffed the milk. Then she sat down before the fish, wrapped her tail about her, and ate and ate until only the bones were left. Then Mitzi drank the milk.

"Did you ever see anything move faster than Mitzi's pink tongue when she drinks milk?" asked Ricka.

All that afternoon Mitzi and the three little girls played together. When Flicka, Ricka, and Dicka went home to supper they left Mitzi asleep in the kitchen chair.

Mitzi drank the milk.

EARLY the next morning Flicka, Ricka, and Dicka hurried over to the little yellow house where Mitzi lived. When they opened the door with the big key, Mitzi came toward them, purring. She walked out into the sunshine.

But at that moment a brown and white dog ran up. Mitzi hissed. The dog barked. Then around the house ran Mitzi, the brown and white dog following her, barking.

As the dog came close, Mitzi ran up an elm tree. Up and up she climbed, almost to the top, for she was badly frightened.

Then the three little girls chased the dog away. But Mitzi stayed in the tree-top all day long, and would not come down. That evening when the children went home for supper Mitzi was still high in the treetop.

Mitzi ran up an elm tree.

FLICKA, Ricka, and Dicka could not sleep that night, for they were thinking about Mitzi in the treetop.

"Perhaps she is hungry and cold," Ricka thought to herself.

Very early the next morning they went back to the little yellow house. They looked in the elm tree. But Mitzi was not there.

They ran around the house calling, "Mitzi, Mitzi, pretty kitty!" But no black-and-white cat came to meet them.

They ran up and down the street calling. "Mitzi, Mitzi." They looked in all the trees for her.

When Flicka met the policeman she said, "Have you seen Mitzi? Mitzi is a big black-and-white cat."

The policeman shook his head, "No."

"Have you seen Mitzi?"

FLICKA, Ricka, and Dicka looked everywhere for Mitzi. They called and called, but no black-and-white cat came to meet them.

"Oh, dear," said Dicka, "why did we ever promise to take good care of Mitzi! Now she is lost."

"Aunt Helga and Uncle Jon like Mitzi so much, too," said Flicka.

When they told Mother about it she said, "Children, you must find Mitzi. You promised to take good care of her, you know."

At last the three little girls climbed a nearby roof to ask the chimney sweep if he had seen a black-and-white cat.

"I couldn't tell the color from here," he grinned, "but I saw a cat run down into that basement."

"I saw a cat run down into that basement."

THANK you, thank you," they said as they climbed down. "We'll look in the basement." They ran down the basement stairs of the house across the street.

"Mitzi," called Flicka.

"Pretty kitty," called Ricka.

"Come here," called Dicka.

Ricka stopped near the basement door. In a dark corner, near a barrel, was a cat with yellow eyes that made noises at them.

Ricka looked at the cat carefully. Then she said slowly, "No, that's not Mitzi. That's a cat we've never seen before."

The three little girls went sadly back up the stairs.

"Where can Mitzi be?" they asked each other sorrowfully.

In a dark corner was a cat with yellow eyes.

WE have looked everywhere," said Flicka. "We've called and called."

"We have looked in the trees, and we have looked on the roofs," said Ricka.

"We even asked the policeman if he had seen a black-and-white cat," said Dicka. "Whatever shall we tell Aunt Helga?"

The three little girls sat down on the doorstep of the little yellow house and began to cry.

"Poor, poor Mitzi," sobbed Ricka. "She's been lost for ever so long."

"We promised to take such good care of her," sobbed Flicka.

Then Ricka looked up.

There on the walk before her stood Aunt Helga and Uncle Jon.

Then Ricka looked up.

YOU haven't seen Mitzi for ever so long?" asked Uncle Jon when the children had told them all about her. "We haven't been gone that long! If you have looked everywhere outside, then she's probably in the house."

"I never knew a cat that liked a house better!" exclaimed Aunt Helga. "There's a basket in my room where she always goes for a long nap. Probably she ran in when you left the door open. Let's go and see. Run ahead, for I walk so slowly."

The three little girls ran into the little yellow house.

When Aunt Helga reached her room, there were Flicka, Ricka, and Dicka gazing at Mitzi curled happily in a basket, with three little kittens!

One little kitten was gray. One was white. And one was black and white.

There was Mitzi, with three little kittens.

IN the weeks that followed it was Flicka who liked the gray kitten.

Dicka always played with the white kitten. But Ricka liked the black-and-white kitten best.

The three little girls and the three little kittens were always together.

"I do believe you hate to leave those kittens to go home to supper," Uncle Jon often laughed.

Then one day Flicka, Ricka, and Dicka had a birthday. Uncle Jon and Aunt Helga came over carrying three little green baskets. In each basket was a kitten.

"Happy birthday," they said, and they gave each little girl the kitten she liked best.

They gave each little girl the kitten she liked best.